BORIS

THE BUTTERFLY AND FRIENDS

BY J T SCOTT

BORIS

THE BUTTERFLY AND FRIENDS

BY J T SCOTT

Bumper the Bumblebee

Boris the Butterfly

Chris the Caterpillar

William and Wendy the Worms

Sally the Sparrow

Kirsty the Kitten

The Three Fish

Gertrude the Gnome

It was an exciting day in the garden.

Post Bumblebee

was delivering an important letter

to **Boris the Butterfly**

inviting Boris to take part in

the **Annual Butterfly Race**.

Boris the Butterfly was fast asleep.

He didn't hear the important letter arrive.

But Boris had visitors

and they knew

exactly what was in the letter.

Bumper the Bumblebee tapped on the window.

"Wake up Boris!" shouted Bumper.

"It's the Annual Butterfly Race,"

said the **Queen Bumblebee**.

"You must take part and enter the competition!"

"Hello Bumper," said Boris.

"How can I win the Annual Butterfly Race?

Everyone else will be really good."

"I've got an idea," said Bumper.

"I could be a butterfly too!

I'll make some big wings and enter the race with you."

“What do you think of my new wings?” asked Bumper.

“I can flutter like a butterfly and take part in the race!”

"No! No! No!" said Boris.

"You can't pretend to be a butterfly.

I will go and ask **Chris the Caterpillar**

and see what he says I should try."

"Hello Chris," said Boris.

"Do you know how I can win the Annual Butterfly Race?

Lots of butterflies are taking part.

Can you help me to win first place?"

"Hello Boris," said Chris.

"Why don't you try eating leaves?

Eating leaves may help you fly faster.

To see if it works, try one of these."

Boris ate one of the leaves.

It made him feel sick

and he turned bright green!

"No! No! No!" said Boris.

"I can't eat leaves to win the race."

“The green colour will fade,” said Chris.

“Eating leaves should make you go faster, not feel sick.

Why don’t you ask

William and Wendy the Worms

for their advice?”

"Hello William, hello Wendy," said Boris.

"I want to win the Annual Butterfly Race.

What can I do to win first place?"

“Don’t tell anyone we told you,” said William,

“but you could use the secret shortcut.”

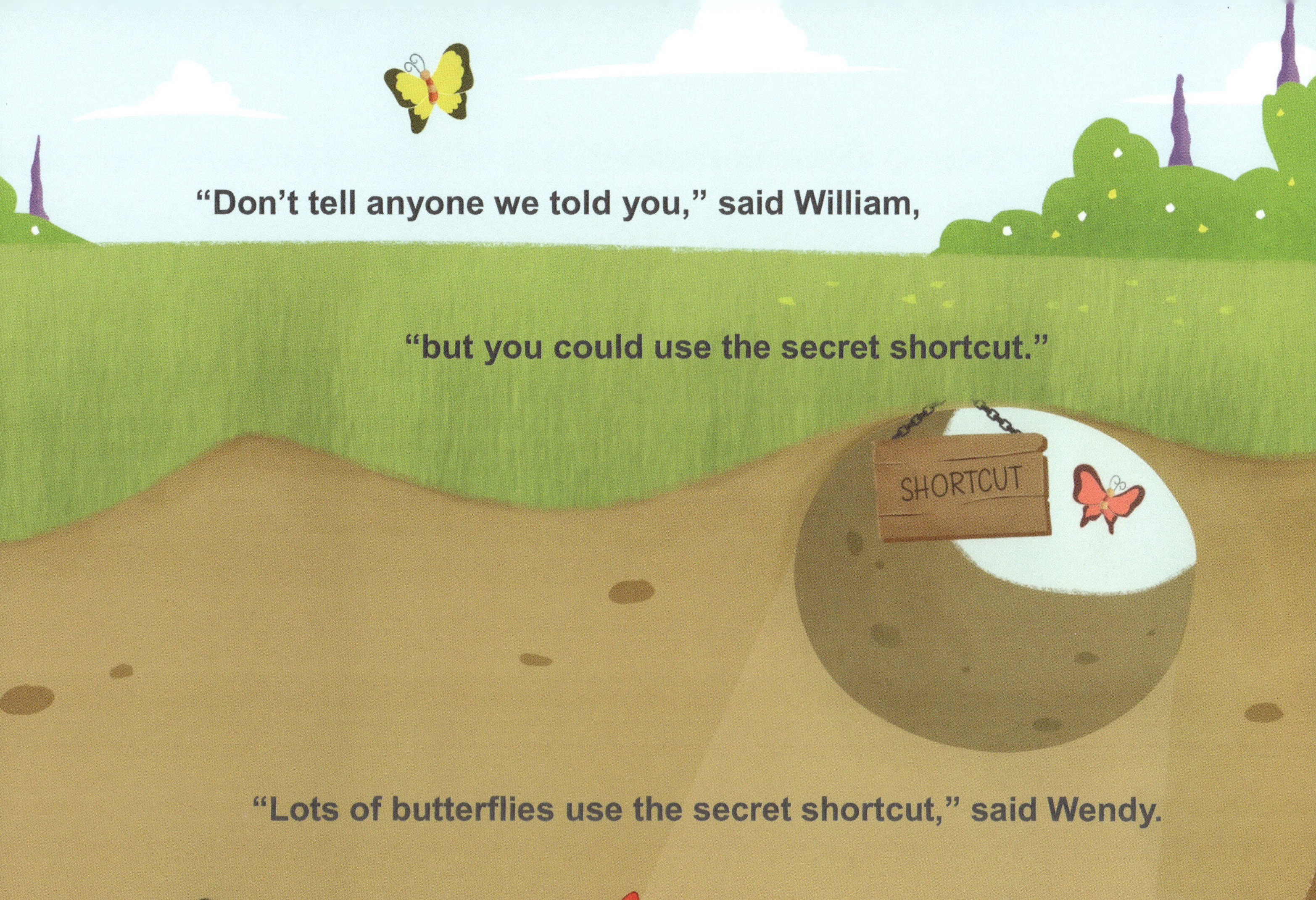

“Lots of butterflies use the secret shortcut,” said Wendy.

“Try it, if you want to win.”

"No! No! No!" said Boris.

"I will not use the secret shortcut.

I want to win, but not by cheating!"

"If you don't want to use the secret shortcut

then you will need to ask someone else," said William.

"Try asking **Sally the Sparrow**," said Wendy.

"Maybe she has an idea that will help you to win?"

"Hello Sally," said Boris.

"I need to win the Annual Butterfly Race.

Will you help me to win first place?"

“I’ve got an idea for you,” said Sally.

“My chicks have made this rocket.

It may help you to win the race.”

"No! No! No!" said Boris.

"I still want to win the race,

but this rocket will fly me into Space!"

"It is a very good rocket," said Sally.

"But if you do not like it,

you must ask **Kirsty the Kitten**

and see if she can help."

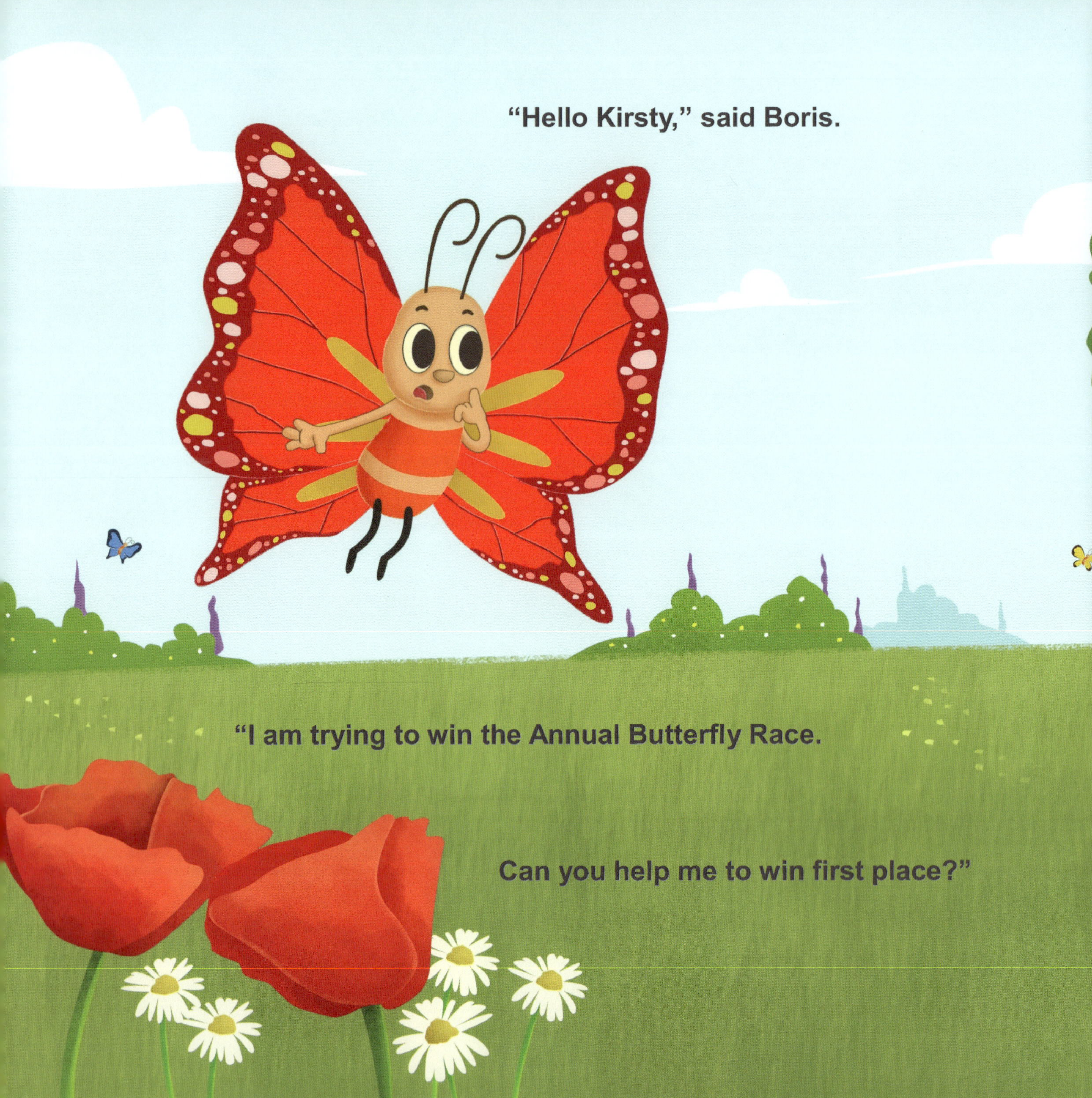

“Hello Kirsty,” said Boris.

“I am trying to win the Annual Butterfly Race.

Can you help me to win first place?”

"Why don't you climb onto my back," said Kirsty.

"I can carry you to the finish line

and make sure you are first."

"No! No! No!" said Boris.

"I can't win by being carried.

No one else is doing that!"

"You are right," said Kirsty.

"Everyone else is flying today.

You must ask **The Three Fish**

and see what they say."

"Hello fish," said Boris.
"I am trying to win the Annual Butterfly Race.
ANNUAL BUTTERFLY RACE
Can you help me to win first place?"

"We blow bubbles

and we swim," said the fish.

"We wish you good luck, but we cannot help you."

"Then what shall I do?" asked Boris.

"I need help from someone to win the race."

"Perhaps you could ask

Gertrude the Gnome

and see what advice she can offer?"

said the fish.

“Hello Gertrude,” said Boris.

“I want to win the Annual Butterfly Race.

I can’t have Bumper pretend to be a butterfly.

I can’t eat green leaves to go faster like Chris suggested.

I can’t take a secret shortcut through William and Wendy’s house.

I can't use a rocket made by Sally's chicks.

I can't be carried around by Kirsty.

The fish had no ideas at all.

I have come to ask for your advice.

Please will you tell me how I can win the race?"

"Taking part is what counts," said Gertrude.

"Go and do your very best.

If you don't try, you'll never win first place.

There's the start line, have a go!"

"Thank you everyone!" said Boris.

"Please wish me good luck!

I will do my very best today

and I will take part in the race!"

A few hours later...

"I've won the race!" said Boris.

"Thank you everyone for your ideas,

but I did it all by myself in the end."

There were lots of butterflies in the garden today.

Did you count them all?

How many did you see?

BORIS

THE BUTTERFLY AND FRIENDS

BY J T SCOTT

Boris the Butterfly and Friends is dedicated to Mum & D2.

First published in 2020

ISBN: 9798649615648

This is a work of fiction. Names characters, places, incidents and dialogues are products of the author's imagination. Any resemblance to actual people, events or localities is co-incidental.

Are you ready for the next adventure?

www.bumperandfriends.com

J T SCOTT

J T Scott lives in Cornwall surrounded by open countryside, lots of castles, pens, paper and a vivid imagination.

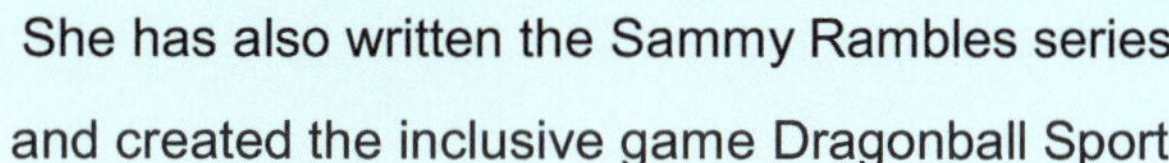

She has also written the Sammy Rambles series and created the inclusive game Dragonball Sport.

Sammy Rambles and the Floating Circus
Sammy Rambles and the Land of the Pharaohs
Sammy Rambles and the Angel of 'El Horidore
Sammy Rambles and the Fires of Karmandor
Sammy Rambles and the Knights of the Stone Cross

www.sammyrambles.com
www.dragonball.uk.com

Printed in Great Britain
by Amazon